# Coping™

# COPING WITH
# ADD/ADHD
# AND ODD

Elisa Ung

Rosen
YA™

New York

Published in 2019 by The Rosen Publishing Group, Inc.
29 East 21st Street, New York, NY 10010

Copyright © 2019 by The Rosen Publishing Group, Inc.

First Edition

**Library of Congress Cataloging-in-Publication Data**

Names: Ung, Elisa, author.
Title: Coping with ADD/ADHD and ODD / Elisa Ung.
Description: First edition. | New York: Rosen YA, 2019. | Series: Coping | Audience: Grades 7–12. | Includes bibliographical references and index.
Identifiers: LCCN 2018012906| ISBN 9781499467130 (library bound) | ISBN 9781499467123 (pbk.)
Subjects: LCSH: Attention-deficit disorder in adolescence—Juvenile literature. | Oppositional defiant disorder in adolescence—Juvenile literature.
Classification: LCC RJ506.H9 U544 2019 | DDC 618.92/8589—dc23
LC record available at https://lccn.loc.gov/2018012906

*Manufactured in China*

# CONTENTS

# INTRODUCTION

ave you ever been so distracted that you weren't able to finish an important exam? Do you often forget where you're supposed to meet friends, or what time parties are scheduled to begin? Do you have trouble sitting still—much more so than your friends? Do you often lose things, such as school books or pencils?

Everyone struggles with these situations once in a while. But they are particularly frequent and troublesome for those with attention-deficit/hyperactivity disorder (ADHD), a condition that affects 11 percent of school-aged people, according to Children and Adults with Attention-Deficit/Hyperactivity Disorder (CHADD).

ADHD is a chronic disorder of the brain that can make daily functioning very challenging. The disorder is divided up into three types: predominantly hyperactive-impulsive type (constant fidgeting, restlessness, and motor-like activity), predominantly inattentive type (forgetfulness and lack of focus), and combined type. It was previously known as ADD, and many people still refer to it as such, particularly when it comes to the type without hyperactivity. However, since 1994, all types have officially been called ADHD.

ADHD can be very stressful, not only for people with the disorder but also for their friends and family. People with ADHD often have problems maintaining relationships and friendships, and have a hard time

Many people with ADHD have trouble focusing for long periods of time, and this lack of focus often hurts their performance in school.

excelling at school and in jobs. ADHD can also make people more vulnerable to substance abuse and other risky behavior, particularly in the teenage years. Many people with ADHD suffer from low self-esteem, particularly those who are not diagnosed.

Two-thirds of those with ADHD are likely to suffer from at least one other "coexisting condition," such as depression, learning disabilities, and anxiety, according to CHADD. One of the most common coexisting conditions is oppositional defiant disorder, known as ODD. An estimated half of all people with ADHD also have ODD, though the condition also occurs on its own. ODD is a particularly disruptive disorder and can make it difficult to function in daily life. Those with ODD can be rebellious, hostile, and argumentative, particularly with authority figures. They may annoy people around them on purpose, blame others for their errors, and defy rules.

Both ADHD and ODD can be hard to identify and diagnose because there is no single laboratory or medical test available for either disorder. Health professionals often rely on screening forms, evaluations, and the observations of parents and teachers. Although many people are not diagnosed with ADHD until their teenage years or beyond, doctors look for a pattern of behavior that goes back as far as childhood.

Once a person is diagnosed with one of these disorders, there are many resources that can help treat and manage the symptoms. These can include medication, different types of therapy and counseling, training, organizational strategies, and academic services and supports.

ADHD does not have to stop anyone from thriving in life. Many people with ADHD go on to become extremely successful, and some say that aspects of ADHD have actually helped them professionally.

# CHAPTER ONE

# Understanding ADHD

Though ADHD is one of the most common chronic childhood conditions, it is widely misunderstood. Its symptoms, its medications, and sometimes even its existence are often portrayed as controversial.

In fact, cases of a mental state with the symptoms of what is now known as ADHD were first recorded in the 1700s, and medical research shows distinct differences between those who have ADHD and those who do not, including how their brains develop and function. A growing amount of research has changed how people understand the disorder over the years. At the same time, the number of people being diagnosed with ADHD— and the number of medications prescribed to them—has grown significantly.

If you think you or someone you know might have ADHD, the first step is to get evaluated by

If you recognize many of the signs of ADHD in yourself or a loved one, it is important to seek medical attention.

a doctor. If you do end up being diagnosed, there are many resources that can help you at school and in your personal life.

## What Is ADHD?

Attention-deficit/hyperactivity disorder is a chronic brain disorder in which people have high levels of "inattention, impulsivity and hyperactivity." Although these symptoms are common in all young children, the difference in those who have ADHD is that their "hyperactivity and inattention are noticeably greater than expected for their age and cause distress and/or problems functioning at home, at school or with friends," according to the American Psychiatric Association.

## The Three Types of ADHD

ADHD is officially divided into three types. A person can be diagnosed with one or the other or a combined type.

- **Predominantly hyperactive-impulsive type:** People with this type of ADHD may not only squirm in a chair but have difficulty staying seated altogether. They may chatter too much, interrupt and volunteer answers before questions have been completed, be excessively "on the go," or act "as if driven by a motor." They may be intrusive in social settings or have difficulty taking turns in a game or waiting in line.
- **Predominantly inattentive type:** People with this type of ADHD may be constantly daydreaming or generally don't appear to be listening. They lose things, are forgetful, have difficulty maintaining focus, and often cannot follow a sequence of

instructions. They find it hard to be organized and often make careless mistakes.

- **Combined type:** People who have this kind of ADHD have symptoms of both types, and this combined type is the most common form of the disorder.

There is some controversy over the first type, hyperactive-impulsive. Some experts believe that it is not its own type and is just an earlier developmental stage of the combined type.

# How Do You Get ADHD?

Researchers say that ADHD tends to run in families. Those who have a family member with ADHD have a greater chance of having it themselves. However, it's not always obvious who has the disorder in their genes. Many adults do not realize that they have ADHD because the disorder was not diagnosed as frequently when they were children. Some parents have been surprised to realize that they have been suffering from ADHD symptoms only after their children are diagnosed and they learn more about the disorder.

Other possible causes of ADHD may include premature birth, low birth weight, injury to the brain, and exposure to lead and some pesticides.

Researchers do not believe that ADHD is caused by a lack of family discipline or poor parenting, poverty or trauma, watching too much television or playing too many video games, or consuming too much sugar. However, these factors can make symptoms worse.

## Can You Outgrow ADHD?

Many physicians once believed it was possible to outgrow ADHD. But researchers now consider ADHD to be a brain condition with no cure, and symptoms can persist into adulthood. Many adults depend on medication or therapy to manage their ADHD symptoms.

## Diagnosing ADHD

Diagnosing ADHD is far more complex than diagnosing, say, diabetes, because there is no quick medical test. There's actually no single test at all. Physicians will often make the diagnosis based largely on the observations of parents and teachers, via screening and diagnostic questionnaires. Some major ones include the *DSM-V (Diagnostic and Statistical Manual of Mental Disorders),*

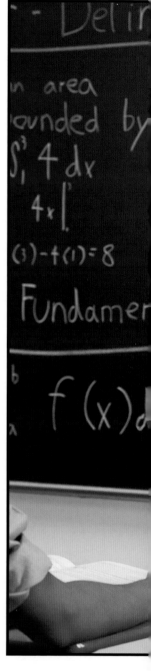

While teachers are unable to formally diagnose ADHD, they are often the first to recognize signs of the disorder in their students.

the NICHQ Vanderbilt Assessment Scales (from the National Institute for Children's Health Quality), and the SNAP-IV (Swanson, Nolan, and Pelham-IV Questionnaire).

Doctors also do medical and psychiatric evaluations and tests to look for—or rule out—other problems that might be causing the symptoms, such as past or present trauma and conditions such as anxiety, oppositional defiant disorder, and learning disabilities. Most people diagnosed with ADHD are of school age. Teachers and other school professionals are often the first to recognize symptoms of ADHD. They deal with many students over the course of their careers so they can pinpoint the ones who behave in a way that is not appropriate for their age. However, teachers cannot diagnose ADHD: that must be done by a medical professional. Many people may start the diagnosis process with their pediatrician or primary care doctor, then visit a psychiatrist or neurologist for more specialized guidance.

## Some Screening Questions

The NICHQ Vanderbilt Assessment Scale is a major screening form for ADHD and some coexisting conditions. Parents and teachers of the child being diagnosed consider a number of statements and say whether these occur "never," "occasionally," "often," or "very often."

# What Role Does Gender Play?

Three boys are diagnosed with ADHD for each girl, according to the National Health Interview Survey (2011–2013). This statistic has led to most ADHD research being focused on boys, and the perception that ADHD is a disorder that affects mostly boys and men.

According to the American Academy of Pediatrics, girls are more likely to have the "predominantly inattentive" type of ADHD, which is not as obvious or disruptive as the hyperactive or combined types. Therefore, teachers and other adults may just consider those girls spacey or moody and do not refer them for testing as often as they refer boys. As a result, girls often go undiagnosed and do not get the help they need. This situation can have severe consequences: the American Academy of Pediatrics say that girls with ADHD struggle more with anxiety, depression, and stress when they reach adolescence and adulthood. They also tend to feel less in control of their lives.

When looking out for ADHD, it's important to look out for all symptoms, not just the most obvious ones, and to remember that ADHD affects people of all genders, often in different ways.

- Does not seem to listen when spoken to directly
- Loses things necessary for tasks or activities
- Is 'on the go' or often acts as if 'driven by a motor'
- Blurts out answers before questions have been completed
- Has difficulty organizing tasks and activities
- Is easily distracted by noises or other stimuli

The full forms can be found at https://www .nichq.org/sites/default/files/resource-file/NICHQ _Vanderbilt_Assessment_Scales.pdf.

## After the Diagnosis

Most medical professionals recommend treating ADHD with a combination of widely established strategies: usually therapy, parent training, and medication. They will take into account factors such as a patient's age, the scope and severity of the symptoms, and whether there are any coexisting conditions.

Because ADHD can impact so many areas of daily life, the American Academy of Pediatrics recommends pinpointing which behaviors are causing the most disruption and developing a comprehensive plan to target them. For instance, is the biggest problem classroom disruption or is it impulsive behavior? Is the person in danger of failing school and therefore most in need of more patience with homework and school lectures? Or is her real problem social skills, and does she need to cultivate better friendships and relationships?

## Is Medication Appropriate?

Medication does not cure ADHD. However, it is often considered one of the first treatments for ADHD, and

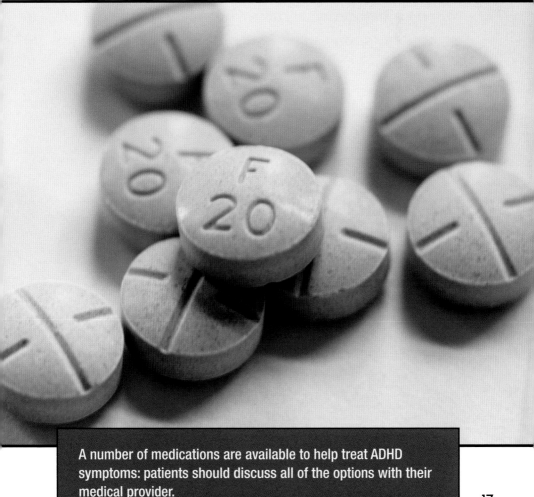

A number of medications are available to help treat ADHD symptoms: patients should discuss all of the options with their medical provider.

the number of medication options have increased over the years. The decision to go on medication can be very difficult for people with ADHD and their families. It is important to collect as much information as possible about the potential benefits and possible side effects and also to consider whether nonmedication strategies can help.

Each person is unique, and only the diagnosed person and his doctor can make the decision about whether medication is right. The process of finding the right medication can be a long one: many medications can take weeks to achieve their maximum effects. It is common for doctors to start one medication at a time at low dosages to see the effects, and to subsequently adjust the dosage.

The following are a few types of medication that are commonly taken by people with ADHD.

## Stimulants

It may seem surprising that these are the most frequently prescribed ADHD drugs—aren't people with ADHD stimulated enough? In fact, stimulants work by helping "important networks of nerve cells in the brain to communicate more effectively with each other," according to CHADD. Ideally, this stimulation results in better focus, less impulsivity, and more ability to organize and plan. This category of medications includes the well-known Ritalin and Adderall, as well as other types such as Metadate, Concerta, and Focalin. They come in short- and longer-acting forms. The most common side effects are a decreased appetite and subsequent weight loss. Other side effects include sleep problems, headaches and stomachaches, tics, and moodiness.

The US Drug Enforcement Administration considers stimulants to be Schedule II drugs, which means they have "a high potential for abuse, with use potentially leading to severe psychological or physical dependence." As with all medications, stimulants should be taken only under the supervision of a doctor.

## Nonstimulants and Antidepressants

These are usually used when someone has not responded well to stimulants or when there is a coexisting condition that may be more effectively treated by a different medication. The most common of these is Strattera (atomoxetine), which helps with inattention, hyperactivity, and impulsivity. Antidepressants, such as Prozac (fluoxetine) and Zoloft (sertraline), are considered to be most useful not for the major ADHD symptoms but for coexisting conditions. And medications such as Tenex (guanfacine) and Catapres (clonidine) are used to address hyperactivity, impulsivity, and insomnia. Side effects include excessive tiredness and dizziness.

## Multiple Medications

With so many people suffering not only from ADHD but also from other conditions, it is not uncommon for doctors to prescribe several medications, usually introducing them one at a time. Ideally, the combination of medications will alleviate many symptoms at once. But side effects must be carefully monitored so they do not make certain symptoms worse.

## Too Many Drugs?

There is a growing concern that many of these medications may be being overprescribed. Some advocates have been crying foul over how pharmaceutical companies have been marketing the drug directly to the general public. According to a 2013 article in the *New York Times*, "The Food and Drug Administration has cited every major A.D.H.D. drug … for false and misleading advertising since 2000, some multiple times." This fact is one more reason to carefully consider any decision to take medication. If in doubt, you can ask for opinions from multiple professionals.

# Therapy, Behavioral Treatment, and Parent Training

"Behavior modification is the only nonmedical treatment for ADHD with a large scientific evidence base," according to CHADD. Major research shows that a combination of this treatment along with medication is often very effective. Some people find they can

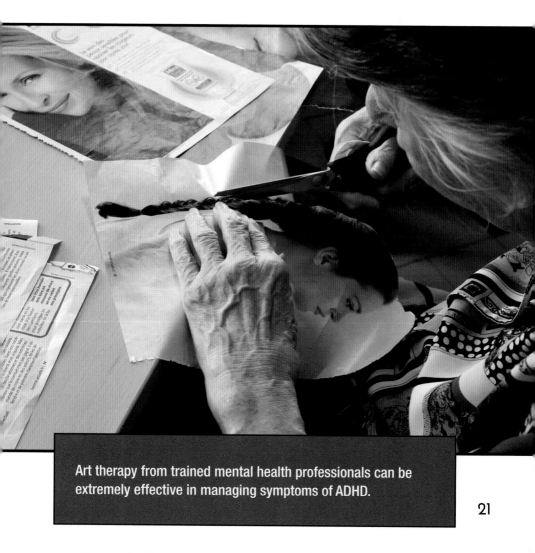

Art therapy from trained mental health professionals can be extremely effective in managing symptoms of ADHD.

21

function with therapy alone, while others decide to start with medication alone. This therapy can be known as behavior therapy, psychosocial treatments, or behavioral intervention. Basically, therapists and other mental health professionals train people with ADHD and their parents to improve their behavior and decrease negative aspects such as hyperactivity, aggressiveness, and noncompliant behavior.

Advocates say this training is one of the most effective ways of helping people with ADHD understand how it's appropriate to behave, resulting in more successful functioning. These treatments can also teach people skills and strategies to deal with symptoms of ADHD, and they can train parents to help their children use these skills. The therapy focuses on triggers, the negative behaviors themselves, and the consequences of those behaviors.

The following are five points of behavior modification as defined by CHADD:

- Start with goals that the child can achieve in small steps.
- Be consistent—across different times of the day, different settings, and different people.
- Provide consequences immediately following the behavior.
- Implement behavioral interventions over the long term—not just for a few months.

Exercise can be enormously beneficial for people with ADHD, and is heavily recommended by medical professionals, as well as some athletes with the disorder.

- Teaching and learning new skills takes time, and improvement will be gradual.

## Exercise

"If exercise could be purchased in a pill, it would be the single most widely prescribed and beneficial medicine in the nation," according to the late Robert Butler, founder of the National Institute on Aging. For those with ADHD, the benefits of physical activity can be tremendous. Not only does exercise improve health, it also increases feel-good endorphins and other neurotransmitters that improve brain activity and function. It requires no prescription, it is drug-free, and it can be free of cost, too. Many doctors will recommend it as part of a treatment plan, and some athletes with ADHD have said that intense bouts of exercise improved their own concentration and hyperactivity.

# Myths & **FACTS**

Myth: ADHD is not real. It's just kids being kids.

**Fact**: ADHD is a very real medical condition widely recognized by organizations such as the American Medical Association, the American Psychiatric Association, the Centers for Disease Control and Prevention, and the American Academy of Pediatrics, all of which note that its symptoms often last into adulthood.

Myth: Having ADHD means you are lazy or unintelligent.

**Fact**: People with ADHD may appear as though they are ignoring instructions or refusing to do longer tasks. In fact, many are the opposite of lazy: they must put in much more effort to finish a task than someone without ADHD. Many people with ADHD are highly intelligent.

Myth: ADHD medications turn people into zombies.

**Fact**: Sleepiness is a side effect of some medications, but often this is temporary or indicates a dosage that is too high.

*(continued on the next page)*

*(continued from the previous page)*

Medication has been proven to reduce ADHD symptoms in many people, and stimulants—the most commonly prescribed ADHD medications—do not usually cause sluggishness.

Myth: My brother can't have ADHD—he can sit for two hours watching a movie.

**Fact**: In a confusing twist, people with ADHD often have no problem focusing on activities that are stimulating and engaging to them. This circumstance causes what some experts call "hyperfocus": a focus so intense that time can actually slip by without the person noticing. Activities rich with visual and audio stimulation, such as video games, movies, and television, can often hold the attention of someone with ADHD for a long time. Something new or novel (such as the first day of school) or something intimidating can also hold the attention of a person with ADHD. The same person may be highly distracted during more mundane activities that require focus and attention, such as everyday school lessons.

# CHAPTER TWO

# Understanding ODD

**M**any people are strong-willed, argue with people in authority, or refuse to obey rules. Some people irritate others on purpose. But those who suffer from oppositional defiant disorder (ODD) are particularly disruptive, often without realizing it. The disorder is one of the most common coexisting conditions in people with ADHD, particularly people who struggle with impulsivity. Alone, ADHD does not generally cause severe aggressiveness or defiance; a long pattern of these types of behaviors often leads to an ODD diagnosis.

## What Is ODD?

According to the American Academy of Child and Adolescent Psychiatry:

> *Physicians define ODD as a pattern of disobedient, hostile and defiant behavior*

*directed toward authority figures ... [T]hose with ODD show a constant pattern of angry and verbally aggressive behaviors, usually aimed at parents and authority figures.*

How do people with ODD act? Not only do they constantly argue and annoy others, they may explode in anger frequently, rebel against any and all rules, be mean and negative, and often seek revenge. ODD most often impacts people in their early years of school, and it is more common in boys. However, it can also strike later and into adolescence, when it affects people of all genders more evenly.

Here are some of the signs of ODD:
- Open refusal to cooperate with major rules
- Constant mean and spiteful talk
- Blaming others for their mistakes
- Deliberately aggravating or upsetting others
- Easily perturbed by others
- Picking fights

If you notice these symptoms in a loved one, it is important to seek the advice of a health care professional.

About 40 percent of children with ADHD will develop ODD, according to CHADD. But ODD is not limited to those with ADHD; it can occur on its own. When someone has both disorders, it can sometimes be difficult to tell where one disorder begins and the other ends. ODD is often more obvious than ADHD because of its level of disruption and explosiveness. People who have ODD as well as ADHD often do

Oppositional defiant disorder is very common in people who have ADHD, and the combination can have a very stressful impact on families.

not respond to common behavior therapy techniques designed to treat ADHD.

## How Do You Get ODD?

ODD is often apparent in a person's nature from birth. These people may have issues being soothed as babies. But other than natural temperament, there are a number of risk factors that can make it more likely that a person will develop ODD. They include having parents who have the same disorder or another mental condition such as depression, having a neglectful parent or parents, suffering severe trauma and stress, coming from unstable or disruptive families, having poor nutrition, and having other mental health issues such as a chemical imbalance in the brain.

Why do so many people with ADHD go on to develop ODD as well? Here is one explanation by Dr. David Anderson, director of the ADHD and Behavior Disorders Center at the Child Mind Institute:

> *Kids with ADHD are biologically loaded to be distractible, to be impulsive, to have difficulty staying in one place for a little while. So kids with ADHD start off doing things that parents perceive as off limits. And then when those kids get negative feedback they start to become even more negatively oriented towards adults.*

# Other Coexisting Conditions

According to CHADD, more than two-thirds of people with ADHD have at least one other disorder, known as a coexisting condition. People become more likely to develop one of these other conditions as they grow older. Oppositional defiant disorder is among the most common of these conditions. The following are a number of others and their prevalence in people with ADHD, according to CHADD.

**Learning disorders** (one in two): These include problems with reading, math, handwriting, and information processing.

**Sleep problems** (one in two): These include issues falling or staying asleep, or sleeping during the day at an inappropriate time.

**Conduct disorder** (one in four): Like ODD, this condition is considered a "disruptive behavior disorder." It includes aggression toward people and animals, stealing, truancy, and other extreme rule breaking.

**Bipolar disorder** (one in five): This mood disorder includes extreme mood swings and outbursts.

**Anxiety** (one in five): Symptoms include excessive worrying, stress, and panicking that interferes with basic daily functioning on social and academic levels.

*(continued on the next page)*

Half of all people with ADHD have a learning disorder. These vary in type and severity, but they often make it very difficult to read and write.

*(continued from the previous page)*

**Depression** (one in ten): This is characterized by sadness, irritability, loss of interest in many activities, constant crying, and sometimes suicide attempts.

**Tourette syndrome** (one in ten): Motor and vocal tics.

**Speech problems** (one in ten): Problems include difficulty pronouncing or articulating words.

Many of these conditions have very different natures. ODD and conduct disorder—along with ADHD—are known as externalizing disorders, which means they are disruptive to other people more than the person who has them. In contrast, internalizing disorders, such as anxiety and depression, bother the person who has them more than others.

## ODD Versus Simple Disobedience

Just like ADHD, ODD cannot be diagnosed by a single test. People with ODD and their parents often start with their primary care physician, who can do medical tests and screening or refer them to specialists. Physicians and mental health professionals

It's common for adolescents to question authority, but those with ODD show frequent oppositional behavior that disrupts their everyday lives.

will want to make sure that the behavior can't be blamed on short-term trauma or another condition. For instance, someone being oppositional or acting out may be doing so to cover up the fact that she has severe anxiety.

Many people can be oppositional in adolescence; in fact, some amount of questioning authority is considered a healthy part of starting to establish independence. Experts looking to diagnose ODD look for the following things: The behavior has been going on consistently for more than six months. It is causing problems in the person's daily functioning. The behavior must be more frequent and intense than is considered appropriate for someone's age. And the anger is usually directed toward an adult authority figure or figures, not peers.

ODD can have a devastating effect on families, damaging a person's relationship with parents. People with ODD are more likely to act out at home or with other authority figures whom they know well. But some bring it into school, ignoring or flouting school rules, which can obviously have a negative impact on their academic career.

According to the AACAP, there is often a gender gap in how ODD is expressed. Although girls may be more prone to lying, boys are more prone to bickering and meltdowns.

# Diagnosing ODD

Experts say that most people with ODD don't realize that they are being oppositional or making irrational decisions. They are often not particularly bothered by their own behavior and do not realize the extent to which their parents and teachers are angry and frustrated with them. Often, those who have ODD believe that their lives are centered around challenging people who exercise authority over them, such as parents and teachers. They often believe they will eventually conquer these authority figures.

In *Understanding the Defiant Child*, psychologist Douglas A. Riley makes a number of observations about oppositional people:

- They are optimistic, believing that they will eventually win at battles such as getting kicked out of school.
- They seek revenge when angered, for instance wrecking their room when they are grounded.
- They "believe themselves to be equal to their parents."
- They frequently respond to questions with "I don't know," because they "often don't seem to like to think."

If these symptoms sound familiar, it is a good idea to reach out to a health care professional for an evaluation.

# Treatment

Because people with ODD often don't realize or understand that they are oppositional, the decision as to whether they receive treatment is usually made by parents or other authority figures. Treatment can include therapy, treatment programs, and medication.

There are many different types of individual and family therapy, including training for parents to help guide the

Some teenagers with severe cases of ODD benefit from being removed from their normal routines for treatment at specialized boarding schools.

person with ODD and improve what is usually a stressful and tense family dynamic. Behavioral techniques and other coping strategies can be taught, and it is often helpful for parents and others to anticipate potentially explosive situations and try to avoid them. Social-skills training can help improve friendships and other relationships.

Another option is inpatient and residential treatment programs and therapeutic boarding schools. Teenagers with severe ODD may be treated in these places, where they are removed from their home, family, and normal routines and immersed in an environment where they focus only on their treatment.

Although there are no medications designed specifically for ODD, people with ODD who also have conditions such as ADHD, anxiety, or depression can benefit from medications designed to treat those conditions.

# Finding a Therapist

People with ODD and their parents may know they need help—for ADHD, ODD, or another condition—but they may be confused about the practical matter of how to get it. ADHD and ODD are often treated by multiple professionals, and those who have never been evaluated for mental health issues may not know what those professionals are called or what they do.

Some logical places to start mental health treatment are a primary care doctor or pediatrician, who can listen to the problem and refer a person to a trusted professional. School counselors, social workers, and psychologists are also good resources, as are major organizations such as CHADD.

The following are some types of mental health professionals, each of whom have their own roles:

**Psychiatrist.** A psychiatrist is a medical doctor who specializes in the diagnosis, treatment, study, and prevention of mental illness. Psychiatrists can prescribe medication.

**Neurologist.** A neurologist is a doctor who treats diseases and disorders of the brain and nervous system. Along with diagnosing and treating ADHD, neurologists can also examine someone for brain injury or seizure disorder, which sometimes overlap. They can prescribe medication.

**Psychologist.** A licensed psychologist can offer therapy for mental and behavioral issues. However, psychologists cannot prescribe medication.

*(continued on the next page)*

*(continued from the previous page)*

**Neuropsychologist.** These are psychologists who look at the relationship between the physical brain and behavior. They often use testing to evaluate people for behavioral and cognitive changes and afflictions. They can diagnose ADHD and distinguish it from other disorders.

**Occupational therapist.** OTs, as they are frequently called, work with people with different types of disabilities to help them perform daily life tasks. Their work includes helping people with ADHD and ODD in areas such as organization and fine motor skills.

# How to Deal with Someone Who Has ODD

It can be very stressful living with a person who has ODD. Experts often offer the following advice to parents and other family members of people with the disorder:

- Be positive and consistent.
- Pick your battles.
- Avoid power struggles.

Mental health professionals advise parents of people with ODD to stay calm, be as positive as possible, and have consistent household rules.

- Set up reasonable rules.
- Be a role model in anger management: try not to lose your own temper.
- Use "what" questions, not "why" questions.
- Try not to take their behavior personally.

If you find yourself struggling to cope with the stress of living with a person with ODD, reach out to a health care professional immediately.

# Long-Term Prognosis

It is essential to treat ODD aggressively because it can develop into a much more serious disorder. If treated, ODD can improve over time. The American Academy of Child and Adolescent Psychiatry reports that about two-thirds of people with ODD who received treatment did not have any symptoms three years later.

However, the people who often struggle with it the longest, according to the AACAP, are those who started showing signs of it in preschool. Studies show that those people are more likely to have symptoms of ODD as they grow older. They also have a greater risk of developing conduct disorder.

Experts say it is essential to treat ODD as early as possible. People with ODD generally do not commit crimes, but if the disorder is left untreated, they have a higher risk of developing a much more serious condition such as conduct disorder. The AACAP says that about 30 percent of people with ODD will eventually struggle with conduct disorder, and that 10 percent go on to develop an even more enduring adult condition such as antisocial personality disorder.

## When ODD Turns into Conduct Disorder

Conduct disorder is a far more severe condition than ODD. It often involves delinquency and extremely dangerous, often illegal behaviors such as abusing drugs; drinking, smoking, and having sex at early ages; and physically hurting others on purpose. The list of terrifying behavior is long: people with conduct

Left untreated, ODD can often turn into the more severe conduct disorder, which often involves delinquent, dangerous, and illegal behavior.

disorder may bully, force others into having sex, attack with or without weapons, skip school, set fires, and run away from home.

The risk of ODD turning into conduct disorder is greater for those who also have ADHD, as well as for those who are raised in unstable families. Also, the aggressive, vicious behavior of conduct disorder can be difficult to treat, and treatment can be long and complicated. People with conduct disorder often have a very difficult time transitioning into adulthood, obtaining and keeping jobs, and maintaining relationships. When left untreated, this condition can often turn into antisocial personality disorder.

## When ODD Turns into Antisocial Personality Disorder

Unresolved conduct disorder can turn into antisocial personality disorder, an adult condition characterized by a general disregard for other people. Some people outside the psychiatric field commonly refer to it as sociopathy or psychopathy. People with antisocial personality disorder lie and deceive others, act impulsively, and hurt people with no regard for their safety or feelings. They may appear charming on the surface, have an inflated sense of themselves, and not show remorse.

This is an adult condition, and people are diagnosed with it starting at age eighteen. Generally, people with antisocial personality disorder displayed signs of conduct disorder before the age of fifteen. It is common for people with antisocial personality disorder to be engaged in violence, criminal behavior, and drug and alcohol abuse. Antisocial personality disorder is considered an extremely difficult disorder to treat, in part because the people who have it are often unwilling to get help.

# CHAPTER THREE

# Coping at Home

There are so many demands on teenagers—academic and social obligations, applying to college, looking toward the future, and more—and the symptoms of ADHD can often get worse during this time. Many people are actually diagnosed with ADHD during their teenage years because the more intense daily demands make their symptoms more obvious. The tendency of people with ADHD to be disorganized and get distracted easily can be a minefield during this busy time. They engage in this kind of behavior because they are typically behind in developing what is known as executive functioning skills.

The home life of teenagers with ADHD can be dramatically impacted by these skills. They may be entering adolescence after a childhood of frustrating behavior and constant criticism. Their relationships with their parents may be constantly

Sports and other activities are often a welcome refuge for people with ADHD, and can be key to happy and productive teenage years.

changing. Increasing demands at home and at school may make time scarce. And parents and children may not see eye to eye on how to handle activities such as watching television, playing video games, and being active on social media.

Plenty of people with ADHD thrive in their teenage years, particularly after they've found a sport, an academic subject, or a hobby that interests them deeply and can be a good funnel for their energy. Developing strategies to structure and organize their everyday lives can help teenagers with ADHD live the lives they want to live.

# What Are Executive Function and Executive Skills?

To understand why it's so important for people with ADHD to have organizational supports and strategies to get through even the most mundane tasks of daily life, it's important to understand executive function. This term means a person's ability to self-manage and self-regulate in order to work toward goals and the future. People with ADHD are often behind in developing these skills, and that's a big reason why the demanding teenage years are so difficult for them.

Here is an analogy to help understand how executive functioning works. Martha Bridge Denckla of Johns Hopkins University School of Medicine in Baltimore compares it to a disorganized cook trying to put together a meal. This fictional cook has an excellent kitchen with all of the necessary equipment,

People with ADHD often lack executive function skills. Experts liken this condition to a disorganized cook who has all the necessary ingredients but still fails to get dinner on the table.

all of the right ingredients, and the ability to read the recipe he wants to make. However, in this case, it does not translate into a meal. Here's where he falls down: he doesn't take all of the correct ingredients out of the shelves and refrigerator, he didn't defrost another ingredient, he didn't preheat the oven, and so forth. That's why he can't get dinner on the table when he wants to.

A person with ADHD might have all of the right skills to function on a daily basis, but he has trouble organizing them and using them at the right time. Imagine how much worse this situation becomes if that person also has a coexisting condition such as learning disabilities (which might give him problems reading the recipe), or anxiety (which could make him panic so that he won't ever produce the meal).

Consider how important this list of executive functioning skills is: working memory (holding information in your head for the present moment), planning, organizing, compiling a necessary list of tasks, activating yourself to start something, maintaining attention to finish it, and controlling yourself emotionally during any setbacks. Research shows that children and teenagers with ADHD do not develop these skills as quickly as other people their age—they may lag by about 30 percent. This delay is a key reason why they have a hard time staying on task while writing, say, a long, tedious book report.

They may not understand the individual steps of the project or how to prioritize them. And they may have a hard time dealing with anger and frustration during setbacks, for instance, if they find out that the book has been checked out of the library.

ADHD is not the only disorder in which people also display executive functioning problems. But these skills are key to understanding what kinds of supports people with ADHD need to make their daily lives run smoothly and efficiently.

## Other Therapies That May Help

While most major ADHD organizations and experts advocate for a combination of medication, therapy, and home organization strategies, many people have found relief from other programs and strategies that do not involve medication.

**Meditation and mindfulness.** Mindfulness—paying close attention to something on purpose—is often recommended as a technique for people with ADHD. This practice can improve concentration and focus and train a person to notice different aspects of a situation. Meditation can help to calm a racing mind, reduce stress, and manage reactions and emotions. There are many books, websites, and apps—such as the popular Headspace—to help with both of these practices.

Salmon, walnuts, and other foods with high levels of omega-3 fatty acids are heart healthy and may help improve some ADHD symptoms.

**Omega-3s and other dietary changes.** Many doctors will recommend increasing the level of omega-3 fatty acids in the diet of a person with ADHD. Some studies have shown that these heart-healthy fats can improve ADHD symptoms, and they are beneficial to general cardiovascular health. They can be obtained through supplements or through foods such as salmon, mackerel, walnuts, flax seeds, and chia seeds. Talk to your doctor if you are concerned about changing your diet. Some people have reported improvement with testing for food sensitivities and elimination diets, though most doctors do not widely recommend these options.

**Biofeedback/neurofeedback/ "brain training."** These are painless brain exercises done by having a person wear headgear with electrodes that monitor brain activity while she plays video games and other computer games. This treatment is often expensive.

Brain Balance. This chain of "achievement centers" has branches all over the United States. Brain Balance is a nonmedical program that aims to help people with not only ADHD but also Asperger's syndrome, autism, dyslexia, and other spectrum and processing disorders. According to the organization, its "integrated approach combines physical and sensory motor exercises with academic skill training and healthy nutrition."

# Time Management and Prioritization

One of the biggest challenges to people with ADHD is the issue of time. They often seem completely unaware of time and have no concept of how long tasks take to accomplish. When they're in hyperfocus, the minutes or hours can slip by without the people even noticing. Meanwhile, they may overestimate the time they spend on activities that are tedious or boring.

People with ADHD often don't know what order to do things in, or how to time them so they're most effective. There are a few strategies that may help with time management.

## Time Routine Tasks

How many minutes does it *really* take to brush your teeth in the morning? Eat a bowl of cereal? Put on clothes? Timing this out, then making a list of the tasks and what order they should be done in, may help to determine an appropriate time to get up in order to have enough time to get ready for school. When your mind wanders, try to bring it back by remembering that you want to get something done in a set amount of time. There are a number of apps to help with this strategy, such as 30/30.

## Make Lists and Keep Them in One Central Place

Writing something down or entering it into a phone means you no longer have to keep it in your mind. Keep your lists in one place: it's so frustrating to have to search for them. You could work with your parents or another adult to consider how important each item is, and maybe even set a deadline that you write down as well.

## Break Up Long Tasks into a Series of Smaller Tasks

Cleaning a whole room can seem like a daunting task, so it's a good idea to try breaking it down into manageable chunks. For example, first put papers away, then put all of the dirty clothes into the hamper, then hang all of the clean laundry up in the closet. Make a list, in order of priority, to avoid getting overwhelmed.

# How Have These Celebrities Handled ADHD?

Before Michael Phelps was a record-shattering Olympic swimmer, he was a nervous, fidgety kid with ADHD who couldn't sit still in class and needed ways to channel his energy. In his book *Beneath the Surface,* he writes that once he discovered swimming, "I felt so free ... I could go fast in the pool, it turned out, in part because being in the pool slowed down my mind. In the water, I felt, for the first time, in control." Eventually, swimming for several hours a day imposed enough structure on Phelps's life that he was able to stop taking stimulant medication. After he eventually became world famous, Phelps and his mother began working to share their experiences and to raise awareness of ADHD.

Many prominent people have spoken out about how they have managed ADHD and become successful in spite of—and sometimes because of—their condition. These people include Olympian gymnast Simone Biles,

*(continued on the next page)*

Four-time Olympic gold medalist Simone Biles has talked openly about taking medication for ADHD, and says it's nothing to be ashamed of.

(continued from the previous page)

Maroon 5 frontman Adam Levine, comedian Howie Mandel, journalist Lisa Ling, actors Jim Carrey and Channing Tatum, conservative TV and radio personality Glenn Beck, and liberal commentator James Carville. That breadth of fame alone shows how people with ADHD can often channel their creativity and high energy levels into stunning careers.

Ty Pennington, the celebrity carpenter from *Extreme Makeover: Home Edition*, was an extraordinarily hyperactive kid and was diagnosed with ADHD in college. He channeled much of that energy into carpentry, art, and modeling. When presented with the challenge of building a house in seven days, Pennington knew it was the perfect challenge for his quick-moving mind.

## Self-Esteem

It is very common for people with ADHD to have a low sense of self-worth. This perception is the result of years of constant criticism about their shortcomings and punishment for their mistakes at school and at home, and it can lead to anxiety, depression, and a loss of interest in learning. These are all things for people with ADHD to be aware of but not dwell on. They can combat these feelings by seeking out environments that allow their strengths to shine. Perhaps this setting could be an art class, music lessons, working at an animal shelter, or even hanging out with others who have ADHD. Those who have energy to burn may find happiness in a sport, theater, or some other kind of high-intensity activity.

# Screen Time

It is striking how people with ADHD who can't sit through a classroom lecture or complete chores can sit for hours watching television or playing video games—particularly ones that move at a rapid pace. Such stimulating activities, rich with sound and visual effects, can send people with ADHD into hyperfocus—such intense focus they block out the rest of the world.

This concentration can have a comforting effect on a temporary basis. It can fulfill a person's intense need for stimulation. It can momentarily block out anxiety, depression, frequent mistakes, and other unpleasantries that are frequently present with those who have ADHD. It doesn't require any of the social skills that people with ADHD are often lacking. Knowing the ins and outs of popular video games and television shows can help them make friends. One company even has a video game in the works specifically to treat the ADHD symptoms of impulsivity and inattention.

Unfortunately, though, most ADHD experts recommend limiting screen time because it can make the symptoms of ADHD even worse. Media can be so engaging and so effective in blocking out the world that hours can go by while homework and other productive tasks get ignored. Violent movies and video games can increase aggressiveness and emotional outbursts in people who are already prone to that behavior. These activities usually involve sitting or being still, and the kind of attention they command doesn't help someone pay better attention in longer, sustained tasks.

Experts say video games and television do not cause ADHD, but people with ADHD should still be mindful of the ways in which they affect their symptoms and behavior. It may be helpful to use a timer to keep track of how long the screen time is lasting and to take frequent breaks. Many parents choose not to keep video games or other screens in the bedroom of someone with

People with ADHD are often particularly drawn to television and video games, but most experts advise against unlimited screen time.

ADHD. Some apps may help with controlling use of electronics: OurPact, for instance, shuts off devices after a certain amount of time.

# Internet and Social Media

People with ADHD have a higher chance of becoming addicted to the internet, which can interfere with social relationships and even with sleep. Social media offers plenty of distractions, and there are huge consequences to being impulsive on social media, where an off-the-cuff remark can be preserved for all to see—and saved for a future employer to dig up later.

In his book *ADHD in HD: Brains Gone Wild*, actor and clothing company owner Jonathan Chesner noted, "You'd be amazed at how many ADHD brains put stuff out there that will have them doing massive damage control later on." A good rule: if you wouldn't want to say something to everyone you know, don't say it on social media.

# CHAPTER FOUR

# Thriving at School

**A**cademic settings are often the single biggest challenge for people with ADHD, and this is particularly true in middle and high school. While elementary school students spend all day in the same class with a single teacher, middle school brings the complication of different teachers, different classes, and the challenge of carrying around books and supplies. This new routine requires skills that are often the most underdeveloped in people with ADHD, who struggle heavily with the new demands of organization, getting distracted, keeping track of time, recognizing how long a task takes, finishing long-term projects, meeting deadlines, and remembering where to go for activities.

In short, it's hard to stay focused in school as a teenager with ADHD! And the coexisting conditions common in people with ADHD

School settings and academics often present enormous challenges for teenagers with ADHD, but there are many resources and strategies to help these teens thrive.

can make this endeavor even more challenging: oppositional defiant disorder can mean problems with adult authority, learning disabilities can make basic academics a challenge—causing people to fall even further behind their peers—and anxiety can be increased by the process of so many transitions occurring on a daily basis.

People with ADHD may have to work harder than most of their peers just to keep up with the basic demands of middle and high school. However, they don't have to do it on their own. With an ADHD diagnosis, they should qualify for some accommodations and interventions that can make academics much more doable. Also, techniques and strategies can help them be more organized.

## Your Legal Rights at School

All students have the right under federal law to be evaluated for disabilities that can affect their educational performance, and to receive accommodations and services at no cost. People with ADHD can qualify for these services, but a diagnosis alone does not guarantee them: ADHD or a coexisting condition must be proven to be adversely affecting a person's academic performance.

The Individuals with Disabilities Act (IDEA), the US federal law that governs special education, covers thirteen conditions. ADHD is covered under "other health impairment." Other conditions include those that frequently coexist with ADHD: a specific learning disability such as dyslexia, autism spectrum disorder, an "emotional disturbance" such as anxiety or depression, and a speech or language impairment. IDEA also mentions blindness and other visual impairments, deafness, hearing impairment, deaf-blindness, an orthopedic impairment such as cerebral palsy, an intellectual disability, a traumatic brain injury, and multiple disabilities.

If you or your parents request an evaluation from your school district, the district will decide whether to order an evaluation, which may include educational, medical, psychiatric, and other testing. If they determine you qualify for special services under IDEA, you will receive what is known as an Individualized Education Program (IEP).

An IEP lists a student's specific issues, the steps to be taken to address those issues, and measurable goals for that student. An IEP can call for specific interventions such as an aide or tutor; a designated special education classroom; speech, language, or occupational therapy; modified tests or homework assignments; and the use of special computer or recording equipment.

Parents are entitled to attend their child's IEP meeting and to obtain a free copy of the IEP itself. Also, an IEP in high school will start to include a transition program to college or other pursuits. Students with an IEP have some protection under federal law for long-term suspensions for violations that are related to their disability.

People who do not qualify for an IEP may instead be eligible for some accommodations and modifications under Section 504, which is a civil rights act that prohibits discrimination against anyone with a disability. These 504 accommodation plans are generally not as detailed or as extensive as IEPs. The 504 plans rely mostly on accommodations and modifications that allow people to function within a regular classroom, such as preferential seating, longer time to take tests, a reduced class size, and different homework assignments.

Some people go through the testing process for these services and disagree with their school's ultimate decision. They may be able to challenge the decision: they can consult attorneys or advocates who are familiar with the ins and outs of special-education law.

# On Advocating for Yourself

Parents are most often the earliest advocates for their children, navigating the world of mental health treatment and special needs programs with their child's best interest in mind. But as people get older, they can start to become their own best advocates. The simplest way to do this advocacy is

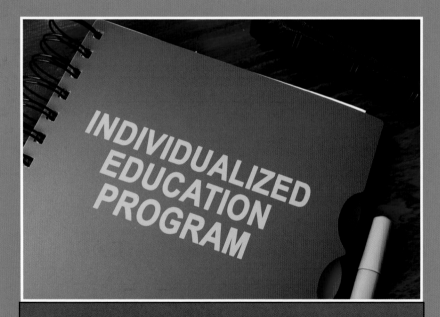

While they may seem dull, IEP meetings are important to a student's success, and teenagers are likely to benefit from attending them.

to ask for help when you need it. You might point out to teachers when you are having difficulty with something and ask for extra help. You can explain to friends where you have difficulties and why, or you can ask an adult to explain to unsympathetic classmates why you need extra time on a test.

Once a student reaches the age of fourteen, she must be invited to attend her own IEP planning meetings. These meetings may be seen as long and boring to someone with ADHD, but they can also help that person learn to advocate for herself, an invaluable skill heading into adulthood and one that may be necessary for those who plan to attend college. If you know what's in your IEP or 504 and why it's there, and you're aware of your legal rights at school, you can point out when they are not being followed. If you can tell your school's IEP team where you are having the most problems, you may get extra support.

## Coping in School

ADHD can make learning in the classroom very difficult. Timed tasks, in particular, can pose major challenges, as can multistep instructions. Although accommodations through an IEP and 504 can help, there are other things to keep in mind.

## Teachers

In his book *All About ADHD*, Thomas W. Phelan recalled a twelve-year-old patient of his who came in with a very scattered report card: an A, a B, a C, a D, and an F. By the boy's own admission, the variability in his grades "was almost entirely due to his like or dislike for the teacher who had given him that grade." Phelan concludes: "My experience has been that kids with ADHD … can be notoriously teacher-sensitive."

Experts say people with ADHD often do well under teachers who are flexible enough to alter their teaching strategies, structure their classrooms clearly, understand and make the accommodations in a student's IEP, and communicate with parents. Students with ADHD often successfully learn with a variety of different teaching methods—not just talking at the students, but also

Teens with ADHD often thrive in school environments where a variety of teaching methods are incorporated into the school day, including music, movement, and visual learning.

including discussion, music, visuals, computers, and various types of movement, including exercise breaks.

## Behavior

For school-aged people whose behavior is not up to the standards of traditional classrooms, their school may ask for a functional behavior assessment. This assessment details problem behaviors, their triggers, and what happens when they occur. This step will often lead to a behavior plan customized to the person's needs. It can include classroom accommodations designed to avoid the triggered behavior, such as a system for breaks during tests and seating away from distracting noises. It can put into place measures to prevent the behavior and provide positive reinforcement.

## Considering Private Schools

Public schools are a good fit for many students. But those who have not thrived in them and have the financial leeway to consider private school may find some that are good fits for the challenges of ADHD. Many private schools have smaller class sizes and fewer students per instructor, as well as an array of nontraditional programs.

## Standardized Tests

People with ADHD can request accommodations when taking standardized tests such as the SAT and

ACT. These accommodations include extended testing time, computer accommodation, and extra and extended breaks. You must provide proof of your diagnosis, show proof of your testing and history, explain your limits of functioning, and draw a clear connection between your needs as someone with ADHD and the accommodations you are requesting. These requests can be made directly to the college board. Find more information at https://www.collegeboard.org/students-with-disabilities/documentation-guidelines/adhd.

# The ADHD Coach

An ADHD coach is not a therapist, a doctor, or a tutor. Think about an athletic coach working to bring out the fullest potential of her students. That's what life coaches do for their clients. ADHD coaches take this activity a step further and have a particular expertise or training in the disorder.

These coaches work with people with ADHD—older children, adolescents, college students, adults, and families of young children—to identify

*(continued on the next page)*

*(continued from the previous page)*

their personal, academic, and professional goals and set strategies to achieve those goals. They help people stay on task and maintain focus in order to achieve their own goals. The clients may be striving to maintain good grades in high school, finish a long project, apply to college, have a more peaceful relationship with their parents, or even just develop goals that will ease them into adulthood.

These coaches generally have a clear understanding of or special training in the challenges people with ADHD face and specialize in helping them overcome those challenges. ADHD coaches say they can help increase executive function skills, self-esteem, and general well-being.

ADHD coaching is most appropriate for people who are already being treated, acknowledge that they need support, and are committed to taking steps to improve their lives. Coaching is typically not covered by health insurance. The ADHD Coaches Organization may be able to help you find a coach in your area.

## Completing Work and Homework

Dealing with homework is often one of the most frustrating parts of having ADHD. Some major

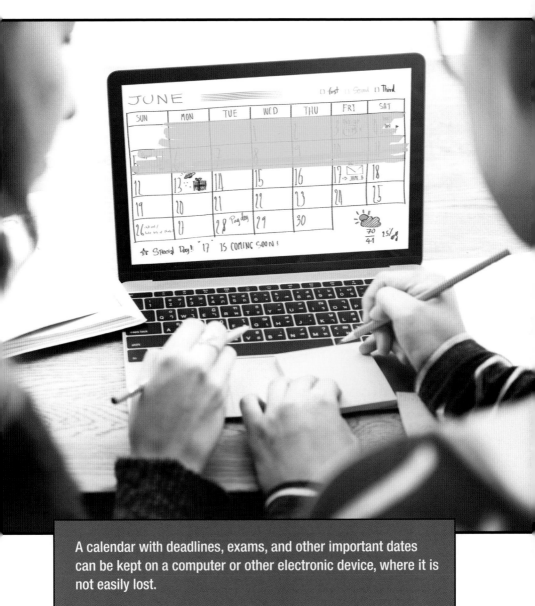

A calendar with deadlines, exams, and other important dates can be kept on a computer or other electronic device, where it is not easily lost.

sources of frustration and the strategies to combat them include the following.

**A calendar.** Whether it's a physical calendar or one kept on a smartphone, laptop, or desktop computer, it's essential to find some formal way to keep track of deadlines, appointments, and other commitments.

**A central place for school supplies.** People with ADHD tend to lose physical objects. Keep supplies and books in the same place, and they will always be there when it's time for homework.

**What are your assignments and when are they due?** Find a way to keep track of everything—perhaps a filing system for assignments, with all deadlines marked on your calendar. Check out the apps that can help with this, such as myHomework.

**Long-term assignments.** Upon getting the assignment, immediately work with a parent or another adult to break it down into smaller parts. Assign a deadline to each part and note it in your calendar.

**A regular clearing-out.** Whether it's daily, weekly, or both, it's helpful to clear out both your desk and your backpack.

**Examine ways of studying nontraditionally and find your best learning style.** The restless nature of ADHD means that some people study better standing up or moving around. Many people have a hard time focusing with background noise or music, while others find they work better with music in the background. Some work better with friends, while some are more efficient at the library or alone in their room.

**Know your ideal focusing time and take frequent breaks.** Apps such as Pomodoro can help by automatically reminding you to take a short break every twenty-five minutes.

**Remember to turn in the work.** Some people with ADHD do their homework but then lose it en route to school the next morning. Make sure the work lands in a designated folder or backpack right after completing it. Ask about the possibility of filing the homework online or emailing it to the teacher.

**Consider a tutor.** Many teenagers have a hard time doing homework with their parents or older siblings. It can be more helpful to study with someone else, perhaps a college student.

**Consider outside support.** Some teenagers with ADHD find it helpful to receive regular check-in phone calls from an outside person who is not a parent or teacher. This outsider doesn't need to be a tutor or a trained ADHD coach—the individual could be a family friend, a friend's parent, your godparent, or your grandparent. This person can simply ask the teenager

Having trouble doing homework or planning activities with your parents? Outside tutors, family friends, or relatives can provide key support.

what her current needs and concerns are, provide help reviewing daily and weekly plans, and provide emotional support and encouragement.

**Medication schedules.** What does medication have to do with homework? Many people who benefit from prescription medications find that their prescriptions need to be adjusted as they grow older. Academic demands are increasing, which may lead to different medication needs.

# CHAPTER FIVE

# Looking Ahead

Sometimes it can be hard to distinguish between typical teenage behavior and some symptoms of ADHD and its coexisting conditions. Many teenagers clash with authority figures, have a hard time starting to date, and have an even harder time trying to learn to drive. They may be prone to addictions with drugs and alcohol. Many teenagers are oppositional.

All of this behavior gets even more precarious when the teenager has ADHD, leaving him on shakier ground than typical teenagers. He may be taking medication that others may want to buy and abuse. Because teenagers with ADHD develop certain skills more slowly than their neurotypical peers, there may be a growing chasm between people who have ADHD and everyone else. The process of preparing for and choosing a college can be overwhelming, as can choosing a career path.

Learning to drive a car is an exciting rite of passage for many teenagers. ADHD symptoms may make it unusually overwhelming.

Many people will still have symptoms of ADHD when they reach adulthood. Although this can be a challenge, adulthood can also be an opportunity to turn many aspects of having ADHD into positives. You can investigate career paths that can minimize your weaknesses and symptoms and emphasize your strengths, areas of interest, and need for stimulation.

You may be surprised to hear that having ADHD can actually help you in many aspects of professional life. Many people with the disorder are exceptionally energetic, creative, inventive, and willing to take risks. All of these qualities are assets in many industries, particularly business.

## Staying Social—and Safe

Why is it hard for people with ADHD to make and maintain friends? They often have a hard time following conversations and paying attention to social cues. They may impulsively interrupt, overreact, and become easily overwhelmed by conversation. All of this behavior can make it hard to make friends. Making and maintaining friendships takes organizational skills just as much as schoolwork. In order to keep friends, you must return their texts and phone calls, set up and arrive at scheduled meeting times, and resolve conflict without turning to angry blowups, aggressive behavior, or physical fights.

## Drug and Alcohol Abuse

People with ADHD have much higher risks for addictions, including drug and alcohol addictions. The low self-esteem that is common among people with

ADHD can make them vulnerable, as can the promise of escape from some of their problems. This situation is complicated by the fact that they are often being prescribed drugs that others abuse, and they may be approached by others to buy or abuse those drugs. It's important to remember that the same drugs that can improve the life of a person with ADHD when prescribed and supervised by a medical doctor can have dangerous consequences when they are abused—not to mention that it is illegal to resell prescription medication.

## Role-Playing

Experts often recommend role-play as a way for people with ADHD to practice being in social situations and to prepare for the temptations of drug and alcohol abuse. To prepare for social situations that may be awkward or intimidating, try practicing small talk. Think about how to start conversations and how to give people compliments and positive feedback. Think about how to respond calmly to criticism or practice walking away from it. You can also memorize sentences that you can say in compromising situations, such as someone asking to purchase your ADHD drugs. For instance, you could say that your parents would immediately notice that the medications are gone.

Teenagers with ADHD may want to change or stop their medication as they grow older. Medical professionals and parents should be involved in this decision.

# Taking Your Own ADHD Medication

Many teenagers do not take their ADHD medication as prescribed. Some dislike the fact that taking medication sets them apart from their peers. They may grow weary of side effects or feel that they can function just fine without it. They may also be upset by the prospect or reality of others asking to illegally buy and abuse it. If you want to stop taking your medication, it is important to discuss this wish with your parents and your doctor, who can advise whether it is safest to slowly decrease the medication instead of just stopping. It's important to monitor the effects of stopping medication on your grades, your progress at school, and your family life.

# Driving

Learning to drive can be one of the most exciting times in a teenager's life, but it is particularly complex when you have ADHD. Being inattentive, distracted, and impulsive on the road can have deadly consequences. People with ADHD are much more likely to receive a moving violation ticket, get into a car crash, and lose their licenses. They are also more likely to be distracted by changing music and texting while driving. Parents of people with ADHD often set limits on the time of day the person can be driving, the number of people that can be in the car, and whether the person needs to take medication in order to drive. Drivers with ADHD should be particularly mindful of always following basic rules of the road and vigilant about taking any prescribed medication.

## Looking Toward College

Federal law requires that IEPs include a transition plan for life after high school. Depending on the student's goals, this plan may include starting work, entering vocational school or college, and living independently. Transition services must be in the student's IEP by the time she turns sixteen. These services may include career counseling, preparation for taking standardized tests, or other related services designed to help the student accomplish her goals. IEPs do not extend to college, but students can be reassessed during the end of high school, and they can take that documentation to college and use it to apply for additional services from that college.

## Transition Plans

Some experts maintain that ADHD can be a huge advantage in the adult world. They note that people with ADHD are often creative, exuberant, charismatic, and original. What comes across as hyperactivity in childhood can be channeled into relentless energy as an adult, and ADHD-ers often thrive in chaos, a quality that can be highly useful in many jobs.

Thinking about your own talents and qualities can be a boon to your self-esteem. Taking steps to delve more deeply into those talents—for example, taking an art or music class or joining a club—can provide some needed stimulation, as well as give you an indication of what you might want to do or study later in life.

Want to work with other young people, maybe even young people with special needs? Look into becoming a teacher. Have a short attention span and want to spend most of your career focusing on one story at a time? Maybe journalism is for you. Like adrenaline rushes, flexibility, and constant movement? What about a career in sales? Want to remain on your feet all day? Maybe the retail or beauty industries are for you.

If you like creating things then moving on to the next thing, you could try the food industry. If you thrive on being in hyperfocus in intense situations, you may look into becoming an emergency response worker. Want to channel that creativity? There are plenty of arts-related professions that need it. If you're fascinated by the body and want a fast-paced job, think about the medical industry. If you need a constant change of scenery, consider driving trucks or joining the travel industry. Do you like to do things your own way? Maybe you'll invent something. Are you impulsive? That's an attribute of some of the best comedians.

Many people with ADHD decide to work for themselves and start their own businesses. This decision allows them to delegate tasks that bore them or that they often don't do well, such as completing paperwork, filing, sending invoices, and other accounting activities, and focus on stimulating things, perhaps the things that keep them in hyperfocus.

People with ADHD thrive in some jobs that allow them to focus on subjects that deeply interest them. Some join the arts and music industries.

# Looking Ahead to College

When applying to college, prospective students can decide whether or not to disclose their ADHD. Studies show that most do not. But doing so will open up accommodations that may be greatly needed. This aspect is particularly true if the student is living away from home for the first time and will be losing the structure previously provided by her parents and high-school IEP.

College is a big transition for everyone, and it is typical to feel disorganized and unmoored, especially for those living away from home for the first time. The business of medication can become much more complicated at a college, particularly if you live on campus. Some university health centers do not prescribe ADHD medication and may not have specific expertise if there is a problem with your medication.

It's not surprising that many people are first diagnosed with ADHD in college. Many of those people have struggled with the symptoms of ADHD but found structure at home with their parents and at school with their teachers. When they go off to college, they have to create their own structure and manage their own schedules, and their ADHD can become far more apparent.

# Going into Business

What is it about ADHD that creates such a high number of successful entrepreneurs? Some of the most successful chief executive officers (CEOs) and businesspeople in the world have spoken openly about how their ADHD helped them start working for themselves and build enormous empires. "Entrepreneurship fits perfectly with the ADHDer's need for stimulation and a willingness to take risks," writes psychiatrist Dale Archer in *The ADHD Advantage*. He notes that anecdotal reports show that "people with ADHD are three times more likely to own their own business." The ADHD tendency toward impulsivity is a key factor here: people with ADHD are often willing to take quick action and take risks that others are not.

David Neeleman, the founder of JetBlue Airlines and several other airline companies, has called his ADHD an asset that helped him come up with pioneering ideas such as forms of electronic ticketing. He told *ADDitude Magazine* that he does not take medication and surrounds himself with staff members who are organized and detail oriented. "I can distill complicated facts and come up with simple solutions. I can look out on an industry with

*(continued on the next page)*

*(continued from the previous page)*

all kinds of problems and say, 'How can I do this better?' My ADHD brain naturally searches for better ways of doing things."

Paul Orfalea is the founder of Kinko's (now called FedEx Office), the printing and business services empire, which he started out of a garage while he was a student at the University of Southern California. He has said that ADHD gave him the ability to see the big picture—that his learning disabilities meant that he was open to finding different strategies to learn and grow.

Selim Bassoul, the chief executive and chairman of Middleby Corporation, a 7,500-employee kitchen-supply maker, told the *Wall Street Journal* that he has ADHD and dyslexia but was not diagnosed until college. He runs his company by focusing on the big picture and doesn't "get bogged down in the details." ADHD, he says, "makes you restless but it can also be a huge motivator for action. It prompts you to go out of the office and into the field. You find yourself constantly on the front line."

Selim Bassoul became head of a huge kitchen-supply maker despite years of struggles in school. Today, he credits ADHD for much of his energy.

## Into the Future

ADHD is considered a lifelong condition. CHADD estimates that about ten million adults have ADHD. Studies cited by CHADD show that at least a third of people who had it as children will still have symptoms as adults. Some adults struggle with basic functioning as much as they did when they were children, and the problems become even more complex when they begin to live independent lives. Studies show that adults with ADHD are at greater risk for certain health problems, are more likely to have injuries and problems driving, have a hard time managing their money, and are more likely to have relationship problems with friends and family.

However, many have learned to manage the symptoms and lead not just productive but wildly successful lives. Many do so because, free from the constraints of traditional schools and studying, they are more able to chose lifestyles and careers that maximize their strengths and suit their natures.

Many adults have gone undiagnosed their entire lives. With more attention on ADHD and other conditions, they may just be learning about the disorder and can start to harness treatment options and strategies to help them fulfill their potential. People who were diagnosed in childhood and adolescence have a big head start on this.

College is often the first place where teenagers learn to live independently. Those who decide to disclose their ADHD status may be eligible for special support.

It's important to remember that, in many ways, coping with ADHD gives people a distinct advantage. They've already had to learn to find untraditional ways of thriving and doing things differently. And very often, they've learned how to work harder than everyone else!

# 10 Great Questions to Ask a College Representative

All federally funded colleges and universities are required to offer some level of accommodations for students with disabilities, but the help itself varies wildly from school to school. Regardless of whether you decide to formally disclose your ADHD, here are some questions to ask a college representative:

1. What are the accommodations available to students with ADHD and other disabilities?

2. What documentation is needed to request such accommodations?

3. What are the counselors and other supports provided to all first-year students to help them through orientation and a transition to campus?

4. What mental health counseling is available?

5. What is the average class size?

6. Where are the quiet, isolated places to study on campus?

7. What types of assisted technology are available—for instance, video and audio recordings of classes, voice-activated software, and computer organization programs?

8. Is there a community of or support group for students with ADHD and other disabilities?

9. Will the health center prescribe ADHD medication? What medical help is available on campus, in case of a problem with medication?

10. Are reduced course loads a possibility?

# Glossary

**ADD** An outdated but still frequently used term for attention-deficit hyperactivity disorder, particularly the type where someone has problems paying attention but is not hyperactive.

**ADHD** Attention-deficit/hyperactivity disorder; a chronic brain condition in which people have problems focusing or are unusually active, or both.

**anxiety** A mental health condition that frequently occurs in people with ADHD; characterized by constant worry, fear, and sometimes panic attacks.

**chronic** Refering to an illness that persists for a long time or reoccurs regularly.

**depression** A mental health condition that frequently occurs in people with ADHD; characterized by a loss of interest in daily life and an overwhelming feeling of constant sadness.

**diagnosis** The identification by a medical professional of what disorder, condition, or disease causes someone's symptoms.

**disorder** An abnormal condition.

**endorphins** A feel-good chemical naturally released in the brain during exercise.

**executive function** A person's ability to self-manage and self-regulate in order to work toward goals and the future.

**hyperactive** Excessively active, sometimes to a disruptive degree.

**hyperfocus** A state of intense concentration in someone with ADHD.

**impulsive** Acting suddenly, without any planning.

**inattentive** Not showing attention.

**learning disability** A brain-based problem with learning at an age-appropriate level.

**neurotransmitters** Chemical messengers that allow signals to be passed between neurons.

**ODD** Oppositional defiant disorder; a persistent pattern of disobedience toward authority figures.

**oppositional** Resisting or refusing to obey rules or requests.

**neurotypical** A person with a developmentally normal brain.

**special needs** The educational necessities of someone who has a disability or disorder.

**stimulants** The most common category of ADHD medication. They work by stimulating nerve cells in the brain to produce more of a neurotransmitter that is lacking.

**therapy** Treatment that is intended to provide relief from or cure a disorder or disease.

# For More Information

American Academy of Child and Adolescent
  Psychiatry (AACAP)
3615 Wisconsin Avenue NW
Washington, DC 20016
(202) 966-7300
Website: https://www.aacap.org
The AACAP offers information on a variety of
  psychiatric topics, including ADHD and ODD.

American Psychiatric Association (APA)
800 Maine Avenue SW, Suite 900
Washington, DC 20024
(888) 35-PSYCH
Website: https://www.psychiatry.org
Facebook: @AmericanPsychiatricAssociation
Twitter: @APAPsychiatric
The APA, which represents psychiatrists and other
  members in academia and research, lists some
  very clear information on a variety of mental
  health issues and their symptoms and treatment.

Attention Deficit Disorder Association (ADDA)
PO Box 103
Denver, PA 17517
(800) 939-1019
Website: https://add.org
Facebook: @adhdadult
Twitter: @adultadhd

The ADDA is focused on advocacy and information on and for adults with ADHD. It offers a free starter kit for adults who have just been diagnosed, as well as an app to record information about your moods, symptoms, medication, and other information.

Canadian Mental Health Association (CMHA)
1130 West Pender Street, Suite 905
Vancouver, BC V6E 4A4
Canada
(604) 688-3234
Website: https://cmha.bc.ca
Facebook: @cmha.ontario
Twitter: @CMHABC
A charity that works to maintain and improve mental health for all Canadians, the CMHA provides information and services, including programs for youth and postsecondary students.

Centre for ADHD Awareness, Canada (CADDAC)
7800 Kennedy Road, Suite 303A
Markham, ON L3R 2C7
Canada
(416) 637-8584
Website: http://caddac.ca/adhd
Facebook: @CADDAC
Twitter: @CentreforADHD

This nonprofit organization focuses entirely on ADHD, supporting and advocating for people who have the disorder.

Child Mind Institute
445 Park Avenue
New York, NY 10022
(212) 308-3118
Website: https://childmind.org
Facebook and Instagram: @ChildMindInstitute
Twitter: @ChildMindDotOrg
This nonprofit is dedicated to transforming the lives of children and families impacted by mental health and learning disabilities. It provides comprehensive and clear information about a variety of mental health issues.

Children and Adults with Attention-Deficit/ Hyperactivity Disorder (CHADD)
4601 Presidents Drive, Suite 300
Lanham, MD 20706
(800) 233-4050
Website: http://chadd.org
Facebook: @chadd.org
CHADD has one of the most comprehensive websites on ADHD, including statistics, information written for teenagers, and information on coexisting conditions.

National Institute of Mental Health
6001 Executive Boulevard, Room 6200, MSC 9663
Bethesda, MD 20892
(866) 615-6464
Website: https://www.nimhgov
Facebook and Twitter: @nimhgov
This research organization, based in the United
    States, provides a wealth of information about
    all kinds of mental health issues.

Understood
Website: https://www.understood.org/en
Facebook: @understood
This website is run by fifteen partner organizations
    and is dedicated to providing information on
    learning and attention issues.

# For Further Reading

Brown, Thomas E. *Smart but Stuck: Emotions in Teens and Adults with ADHD.* San Francisco, CA: Jossey-Bass, 2014.

Burdick, Debra E. *Mindfulness for Teens with ADHD.* Oakland, CA: New Harbinger Publications, 2017.

Chesner, Jonathan. *ADHD in HD: Brains Gone Wild.* Minneapolis, MN: Free Spirit Publishing, 2012.

Hansen, Sharon A. *The Executive Functioning Workbook for Teens: Help for Unprepared, Late, and Scattered Teens.* Oakland, CA: New Harbinger Publications, 2013.

Melmed, Raun. *Melvin's Monster Diary: ADHD Attacks! (But I Rock It, Big Time)* Sanger, CA: Familius LLC, 2016.

Nagelhout, Ryan. *Michael Phelps: Greatest Swimmer of All Time.* New York, NY: Rosen Publishing, 2018.

Phelps, Michael, with Brian Cazeneuve. *Beneath the Surface: My Story.* New York, NY: Sports Publishing, 2016.

Shankman, Peter. *Faster Than Normal: Turbocharge Your Focus, Productivity, and Success with the Secrets of the ADHD Brain.* New York, NY: TarcherPerigee, 2017.

Shea, Therese. *Teen Mental Health: ADD and ADHD.* New York, NY: Rosen Publishing, 2014.

Taylor, John F. *The Survival Guide for Kids with ADHD.* Minneapolis, MN: Free Spirit Publishing, 2014.

# Bibliography

American Academy of Child and Adolescent Psychiatry. "What Is ADHD?" Retrieved February 28, 2018. https://www.aacap.org /aacap/Families_and_Youth/Resource_Centers /ADHD_Resource_Center/ADHD_A_Guide _for_Families/What_is_ADHD.aspx.

Archer, Dale. *The ADHD Advantage: What You Thought was a Diagnosis May Be Your Greatest Strength.* New York, NY: Avery, 2015.

Branstetter, Rebecca. *The Conscious Parent's Guide to ADHD.* Avon, MA: Adams Media, 2016.

Brown, Thomas. *Attention Deficit Disorder: The Unfocused Mind in Children and Adults.* New Haven, CT: Yale University Press, 2006.

Centers for Disease Control and Prevention. "Attention-Deficit/Hyperactivity Disorder (ADHD): Basic Information." May 31, 2017. https://www.cdc.gov/ncbddd/adhd/facts.html.

Center on the Developing Child, Harvard University. "Executive Function and Self-Regulation." Retrieved March 5, 2018. https:// developingchild.harvard.edu/science/key -concepts/executive-function.

Children and Adults with Attention Deficit-Hyperactivity Disorder (CHADD). "About ADHD." Retrieved February 28, 2018. http:// chadd.org/Understanding-ADHD/About -ADHD.aspx.

Ehmke, Rachel. "What Is Oppositional Defiant Disorder?" Child Mind Institute. Retrieved March 1, 2018. https://childmind.org/article /what-is-odd-oppositional-defiant-disorder.

Frank, Michelle. "ADHD: The Facts." Attention Deficit Disorder Association. Retrieved February 28, 2018. https://add.org/adhd-facts.

Gilman, Lois. "How to Succeed in Business with ADHD." *Additude Magazine*, December 2004 /January 2005. https://www.additudemag.com /adhd-entrepreneur-stories-jetblue-kinkos -jupitermedia.

Phelps, Michael, with Brian Cazeneuve. *Beneath the Surface: My Story*. New York, NY: Sports Publishing, 2016.

Reif, Sandra F. *How to Reach and Teach Children and Teens with ADD/ADHD*. San Francisco, CA: Jossey-Bass, 2016.

Reiff, Michael I., and the American Academy of Pediatrics. *ADHD: What Every Parent Needs to Know*. 2nd ed. Elk Grove Village, IL: American Academy of Pediatrics, 2011.

Riley, Douglas A. *The Defiant Child: A Parent's Guide to Oppositional Defiant Disorder*. Lanham, MD: Taylor Trade Publishing, 1997.

Schwarz, Alan. "The Selling of Attention Deficit Disorder." *New York Times*, December 14, 2013. https://www.nytimes.com/2013/12/15/health /the-selling-of-attention-deficit-disorder.html.

Shankman, Peter. *Faster Than Normal: Turbocharge Your Focus, Productivity, and Success with the Secrets of the ADHD Brain.* New York, NY: TarcherPerigee, 2017.

Silverman, Rachel Emma. "How a CEO with Dyslexia and ADHD Runs His Company." *Wall Street Journal*, May 16, 2017. https://www.wsj .com/articles/how-a-ceo-with-dyslexia-and -adhd-runs-his-company-1494952535.

# Index

internet addiction, 62

## L

learning disabilities, 6, 14, 31, 50, 65–66, 93

## M

medication, 16, 17–20, 22, 25–26, 37, 38, 39, 51, 79, 85, 90, 97
side-effects, 19, 20, 25–26, 85
mindfulness, 51

## N

Neeleman, David, 91, 93
neurologists, 14, 39
NICHQ Vanderbilt Assessment Scale, 14, 16
nonstimulants and antidepressants, 19–20
nutrition and diet, 30, 53, 54

## O

occupational therapy, 40, 67
omega-3 fatty acids, 53
oppositional defiant disorder (ODD), 14
coexisting with ADHD, 27, 28–29, 30–31
dealing with people who have, 40–41
definition, 27–28
diagnosing, 33, 35, 36
diagnosis difficulties, 6
effects on family, 35
and gender, 28, 35
long-term prognosis, 42–45
problems with adult authority, 6, 28, 35, 36, 65
risk factors, 29–30
symptoms, 6, 28, 35
treatment, 7, 37–40
versus simple disobedience, 33–34

## About the Author

Elisa Ung is an award-winning writer and veteran journalist whose keen interest in ADHD and its coexisting conditions stems from watching their impact on family members. Formerly a news reporter for the *Philadelphia Inquirer* and a columnist for *The Record* and northjersey.com, she is a graduate of the University of Southern California's Annenberg School for Communication and Journalism.

## Photo Credits

Cover Natalia Solovii/EyeEm/Getty Images; pp. 5, 12–13 Ariel Skelley/DigitalVision/Getty Images; pp. 9, 41, 47, 78–79, 95 Monkey Business Images/Shutterstock.com; p. 17 Chris Gallagher/Science Source/Getty Images; p. 21 BSIP /Universal Images Group/Getty Images; p. 23 Lee Torrens /Shutterstock.com; p. 29 JGI/Jamie Grill/Blend Images /Getty Images; p. 32 LiliGraphie/Shutterstock.com; p. 34 Ryan McVay/The Image Bank/Getty Images; p. 37 Tom Merton /Caiaimage/Getty Images; p. 43 Larina Marina /Shutterstock.com; pp. 48–49 SnowWhiteImages /Shutterstock.com; p. 52–53 Kerdkanno/Shutterstock.com; p. 57 Petr Toman/Shutterstock.com; pp. 60–61 Samuel Borges Photography/Shutterstock.com; pp. 64–65 cheapbooks /Shutterstock.com; p. 68 designer491/Alamy Stock Photo; pp. 70–71 Gideon Mendel/Corbis News/Getty Images; p. 75 Rawpixel.com/Shutterstock.com; p. 81 Arthur Tilley /Stockbyte/Getty Images; pp. 84–85 Niedring/Drentwett/Alloy /Getty Images; pp. 88–89 track5/E+/Getty Images; p. 92 Khaled Desouki/AFP/Getty Images.

Design and Layout: Nicole Russo-Duca; Editor: Rachel Aimee; Photo Researcher: Ellina Litmanovich